JUST SPEAK IT!

by

Ingrid E. Bridges

LIFE TO LEGACY

Just Speak It
By: Ingrid E. Bridges, Copyright © 2019

ISBN 13: 978-1-947288-45-4
IBSN 10: 1-947288-45-8

Printed in the United States
10 9 8 7 6 5 4 3 2 1

Cover design by: Legacy Design Inc.
                   legacydesigninc@gmail.com

Published by:
Life To Legacy, LLC
20650 S. Cicero Ave, #1239
Matteson, IL 60443
(877) 267-7477
www.life2legacy.com

CONTENTS

DEDICATION

To my wonderful father, who taught me to never give up on my hopes and dreams, no matter how large or small.

All Things are Truly Possible, If…

WHATEVER YOU THINK TO BE IMPOSSIBLE, IN MOST CASES, is possible. Remember the adage, if you can see it, then just speak it into existence. Well possibility runs on that same track my friend.

Just saying positive statements, may sound far-fetched, even unbelievable. In secular circles, it's called "positive thinking" or "speaking good" into existence, but, biblically, the written word says, "all things are possible with God."

And yes, all things are possible when almighty God plays an intricate part of whatever there is on the horizon. God has all power. He is all nurturing and has all substance within His hand. Just a small touch from Heaven's door, anything, I mean anything is surely possible.

Imagine this, if there was a dimension when all humanity finally realized, God's plan is divine, a plan that works without any assistance from human hands, human ideas, human forethought. Nothing on this earth can compare nor compete with such an outcome. What would man do if this happened? Could this be conceivable, or acceptable on ordinary terms? No.

Everything in existence began from someone's idea, someone's thought, someone creating it on this earthly plane, but then there is one simple complexity – in which man seldom takes time to realize. There is a God. An almighty God who made all things for the good of the land, so who induces a simple thought? He does.

So, why not start believing that whatever you have on your mind that is negative, dark, sublime, ordinary, simplistic or is out of sync with His plan for your life. Seeking the creator for your next move is completely different than seeing a physician about your aches and pains or consulting a dentist about a painful toothache.

All things, I mean all things are possible when God says "yes" even when man says "no." When Moses climbed Mount Sinai, seeking God's face, he was met with no human face, no human body, no man standing against a fence. Instead, God spoke to Moses, directly as a spirit. There was no computer screen with instructions for the Hebrew slave to follow, instead, he was instructed with a few keen words from His heavenly father. Simple instructions.

Those instructions were not mere words. Yet, each word were powerful action words. Words are swords for battle, leading to steps to unknown territories.

Once there was a man, named Arthur who had a problem on his job. A problem that kept him up at night. His manager seem to belittle him before others his staff, every chance he got. The man was so tired of this type of behavior that he began to suffer headaches, over it. One day his sister, Jean, who lived out of town called to see how her big brother was coming along. She noticed his voice wasn't upbeat, she said "what's got you down?" He told her what was going on. Jean said, "You don't have to take all of that mistreatment. Like I always do, I pray about. I tell God all about it, asking Him to fix it the problem. You know whatever we confess to God, He is a wonderful, mighty God who takes care of us, when we are being attacked."

Arthur responded to his sister, " You know I will do it." She told him to speak life over the situation, and know that whatever you profess God hears you and then, step back. Trust that God will do the rest."

He felt better after speaking to his wise sister, who was also a victim of ill witted forces on her job a few years back. She learned how to use her inner wisdom, her relationship with God, and her belief in a higher power to fight her battles.

Jean told her brother to pray for new peace on his job and reminded him to do like they did when they wanted something from their parents when they were kids. Keep saying what you want, until it happens. He thought about it and said to himself, "what do I have to lose."

As the good book, the Bible says, *"God makes all grace abound toward me so that I always have all sufficiency and an abundance for every good work."* (2 Corinthians 9:8)

So each morning, Arthur said," I will not be taken for granted, instead, I will rise above all things, dark, negative and demeaning. I will not be defeated, I got the victory. I trust you God to see me out of this dilemma."

For it is written, *"I ask God to set a guard over my mouth. He keeps over the door of my lips."* (Psalms 141:3)

After trusting in God to take care of the situation, it wasn't two months that had passed before Arthur saw

God's hand move on his situation. That belittling boss was offered a better position in another department and Arthur was offered his job. Hooray!

So you see, Arthur did not only pray about his situation, he also spoke life over it. He spoke victory over his circumstance. He looked at his situation as a project that only God could complete. In the end, Arthur harnessed just what he declared and what he decreed, the victory.

No matter who you are, where you live, what your background is or isn't "you (can) have whatever you speak into the atmosphere," for the good book says, that "anything is possible with God," I mean anything. For it is God's great pleasure to "bless you" be it your deepest desires, even old and new dreams, too.

The real question is, do you believe that your heavenly Father wants to make that which seems impossible in your life, a resounding possibility?

Since mankind began life's journey on God's great earth, man's thoughts began to serve as a huge incubator for everything surrounding him, and those things never dreamed of. Every tiny thought, every brilliant idea, or every whimsical day dream eventually became an astounding possibility.

When Adam, the first man, thought about human nourishment, initially it first started with a thought. Yes, he thought about it. He saw it in his mind, by probably pondering how to make those deep thoughts a living possibility. Was it a miracle that God gave man direction on how to plant seeds to grow fruits and vegetables for nourishment? Yes.

Man, either saw, thought about it, then, eventually spoke it into fruition–probably by saying to himself, "I got to find more of this stuff, so I can survive."

The creator, almighty God, provided every seed for mankind, even a place to plant the seeds, in return humanity could enjoy all kinds vegetables and fruits to eat and grow strong, in today's world.

Stemming back as far as the days of Adam's garden experience–to the obedience of the world's first ship master, Noah, to the philosophers of old like Aristotle to the wonderment age of Nietzsche's selfish writings, to the memoirs of the late President John F. Kennedy, who pronounced that man would one day walk on the moon, man imagined it first. Mind you, in 1968, man surely walked on the moon. They all spoke their thoughts, ideas and dreams into reality.

Yesteryear's magnificent thinkers brought life to their thoughts by reaching a little further than those who hoped for it. They had an itch that kept itching, thoughts they constantly repeated, even seeing glistening stars shine that others could not see. They did more than recant, they acted upon what they were feeling deep down inside of them.

Today, well, we can recall, reminisce, even reflect upon their spoken words, read their journals, behold their written thoughts that so profoundly help shape the world we now live in.

Only a few short years ago, I heard some powerful words of assured possibility spoken by the 44th President of the United States of America, Barack Obama. His ideology of "yes we can" broke records in the first term of his presidency.

President Obama once stated that, "with all Americans working together as a family, as a collective community, this nation could possibly eliminate the current economic crisis affecting millions of home owners, single parents, veterans and disabled individuals." How did the economy bounce back? Consequently because of his enduring words, "yes we can" people were inspired. Those three words poured confidence over defeat. Broke the ice barriers of the times that were freezing above and beneath people's lives.

Since President Obama's life changing words roamed mother earth, Americans reaped rousing results. Unemployment went down, banks became stabilized, the automobile industry bounced back, healthcare became available for millions of people who had none, and millions began to have hope in the American dream once again. This grass roots leader spoke possibility with relentless confidence and might. Because of his tenacity to trust his words, millions of lives slowly began to be better in astounding ways, big time.

For centuries, powerful sure-footed words were spoken by countless men of valor, as well as some of the world's most determined women have shaped vast cultures for the greater good. Across America, words of possibility helped changed people's civil rights and human rights. These individuals probably had great ideas, which in turn became a reality after "just speaking" greatness into existence for the betterment of all humanity.

What did these great leaders do? They thought it, they spoke it, they saw it too, and presto...great change occurred. A much needed change which gave women equal rights; change which gave all people of all races, creeds and religions renewed dignity to do the impossible; to make the impossible, a possibility.

Techniques, Tools and Elbow Grease

No one would imagine how much these individuals faced with countless setbacks, numerous roadblocks, vile opposition, even derailments at times, but they forged forward toward their goals. It was their determination to change what appeared impossible into reality.

Dreams do come true if a person believes hard enough. Believing that what seems, useless, could indeed become a home run.   Usually, a person must put in some hard work to get things done.

Hard work pays off, no matter what your project might be. No one reaches the pinnacle of success without having a few set backs, but, if they are determined enough, they can reach the mountain top and so can you.

No mountain is a slope or an hill. The mountain represents, height, depth, vision, persistence and overall, over coming all obstacles. In order to surpass your greatest fears, you must be persistent in your craft. You understand that you have to give your plan your all. You might begin slowly but then you will be working so hard that your time seems minimal. Your days will seem like mere minutes, because you are finally using your time not foolishly but with a spirit of all willingness and divine purpose.

You realize that what you have been professing for years can be yours, if you put your mind, your heart and your soul into it. First, you must not only speak about, but also write down your idea, write your plan, stick to your outline, and conclusion. Putting every step down on paper will help insure that you will not forget what is necessary to attain that in which you are now professing to do.

No matter how long it takes for you to conquer your fears, you have to work that plan that you created. And it is because you are determined to have what you profess, by taking time out each day to declare that thing, to decree that thing, it is only a matter of time and energy, you will succeed.

Success will not be yours unless you use your time wisely. Time is money. Time is an endless clock that allows you to spend it however way you wish. So when there is a goal in mind, you have to use your time to benefit you, even if life appears to be passing fast in front or in back of you.

Use every empty moment, every passing unused hour to work your plan. If you have children, set aside a few hours for you to work your plan. Hire a baby sitter if need be. If you are working a job, make sure you set aside a few hours maybe three days a week, to work your plan. Remember your time is important when you are proclaiming victory over your goals, your plans.

Tell yourself I can do this thing. Set in your mind that you can work one plan at a time. Make sure you speak powerful words over every little detail, every day. Say to yourself, I can, and I will succeed like so many who once felt defeated but are now on top of the world.

There once was a lady named, Marlene, who cared for her ailing parents while studying for the bar exam. She had always wanted to be a lawyer, but family matters seem to always come up while she was in graduate school. Being the eldest child, she knew her younger sister, who was modeling in New York, wasn't in any shape to care for their parents. So she took up the slack, putting her own plans on the back burner while she worked as a book keeper at her uncle Bert's furniture store. The job paid well, but had long hours especially at the end of the month. She had payroll to do for 15 employees and other office duties. Daily she had to open up and close the factory, sometimes late at night.

One day her uncle Bert asked her if she had a date for company's upcoming 30th anniversary dinner. Marlene, said, "Are you kidding, I barely have enough time for myself. When I'm done taking care of mom and dad, I try to find time to study for the bar exam. At times, I feel like I'm walking in sand to accomplish my dreams. So no, who wants to date a tired lady, with half met goals," she added.

After hearing those defeating words from his favorite niece, Bert had a wonderful thought, he told her, "Take the next few weeks off on me," he said. "I have my old friend coming in for the anniversary event and she always hints that she wants to help me with the business. I'll have her do the books and run things around here while you get your life back on track. She use to be my office manager back in day. It'll be fun," he said.

Marlene could not believe that her uncle was being so understanding. She thought about it, thinking how she never told anyone about how over-whelmed she was feeling. But, she recalled that it was just the Sunday before, that she prayed to God for a better way to accomplish her goals. She remember asking, God to give her the tools to make it happen.

Although, Marlene was putting in the hard work, she felt defeated. It wasn't until she prayed an earnest sincere prayer, that her breakthrough came in a form of free time. Remember time is a magnificent wonder. Using your time with perfected planning, will make hard work seem like a hobby when you look back at how wisely you used it.

Every moment you spend on making your plan a reality, learn to trust God to give you the energy to conquer those hopeless feelings, that kept you from getting started on making a new you. No one who has ever succeeded in their life purpose, did it over night, so know that hard work will always pay off big time.

Pray over your plans and trust God to give you the strength to work it. No matter how tired you get in the process, always look at the finish line. Remember the mountain top has your name on it, if you are willing to take out the time in to make it yours.

What techniques or gimmicks did these unique individuals' practice that eventually allowed them to have such an effective mind-set that others have since benefited? Did they have a specific road map, maybe, a magic wand or descriptive list to follow?

No. Simply no, and, no again.

They put made a conscience decision to soar, to accomplish their dreams. They knew they had to pull up their sleeves and get busy working hard toward making their ideas, a reality. Looking at the cup overflowing instead of half full was no longer a part of their thought pattern.

Today, people of all walks want to be like someone rich, successful or just exceedingly assertive, but lack know how. Still people of great success had to endure great lengths by working harder than most people who dream great dreams. Despite how others want to imitate those who have succeeded in different realms of life, hard work reaps great benefits. For some, harnessing a sense of eagerness like old century wise men did is easy because they found the tools to succeed in time, but for those with get rich quick schemes, found they were constantly not hitting but missing their mark.

In the turn of the 20th century, the industrial revolution created countless wealthy inventors. Thousands of people who were eager yet lacked technique their lack of faith failed them. Some were wise enough to adopt another's mannerism, record their words, repeat every powerful word they spoke, they wrote or held their words close to their hearts. Why? Because they spoke words that moved mountains, not only for them, but for all who are like them.

Let's imagine what words were spoken by great men of yesteryear... many spoke in places where resources, such as encyclopedias, research books, even dictionaries were obsolete. Some of these great leaders, many who were philosophers, biblical titans, even great educators as well as inspirational women, all spoke from their hearts, not from their cuffs.

Each one of these enchanting individuals were peculiar, unique vessels of their times. They were chosen to suit the shifting mounts of those times. Possessing a gift; each had a God given gift in common which made them similar in theory. They all just spoke what they believed would become a possibility. They never depended on doubt as their leaning post. Such mirrors of reality appear to be as unfolding as the universe... however, their words worked miracles!

Looking back, these powerful words not only had profound meaning then, their words are like gold even in modern times. Times where the internet, social media, Webster's Dictionary is abundantly available. Daily powerful words were quoted, unsurmountable statements were taken into account, and every small thought or idea was studied. People began to just speak life over death, truth over defeat, honor over dishonor.

SPOKEN WORDS ARE KEY

Your powerful life changing words are waiting to be just spoken. Hidden within you, within your mind are ideas, words, and meaningful thoughts of power. These gems are floating within you, probably cascading in unknown territories of your sub-conscious for years. If spoken with a new surge of confidence, such words could guide you further than you ever dreamed. Like those dreamers of old, your words are like small keys to an unseen place waiting to open doors to new places, unventured, unseen.

Mind you, words carry energy. Some give life, some take life away. Using power-driven words are like using new keys to unknown doors where unseen realities await you. Those doors are abundantly waiting in a vast forest where your deepest desires and dreams lay dormant. Choosing to place your feet in arenas you've never imagined will take a new way of speaking power into your life.

Every doorway leads somewhere. To another room, an office, a washroom, a bedroom or hallway where there is another doorway to somewhere unknown. In life, you will enter in and out of many doorways, for business, legal matters or in your personal life.

Imagine speaking new doorways into your life. Places you want to venture into, places you only dream of when the world seems like a boring place. You saw it first in your day dreams. Every idea starts with a thought. What if you spoke your thoughts of new places you want to venture to, over and over again, every morning?

Your thoughts serve as keys to places unventured, unheard of. You speak about, you think about, you tell yourself "I can do that" and you will. Your words are not only keys to your success, each one spoken by you, says much about who you are, and who you feel you are. Choosing your words carefully, means more than just saying something, each word serve as a key to unlock new doors, new places and a new you.

Telling yourself you are ready to mount up like an eagle to take the world in your hands, can catapult you to any level, if you believe it. Using certain words as keys to your success, can change your life direction in an instant.

While attending a birthday dinner, a vegetarian declared that he was not going to speak or think one thing negative or derogatory for 30 days. His words astonished those at the dinner table, because they thought it was a vegetarian exercise. He said no, that it was a mind changing exercise.

"What will this accomplish?"asked one of the dinner guest. "This will make anyone who uses this exercise, to instantly have a clearer mind to see the world differently. Where those old cob webs that make people procrastinate about doing this or doing that will leave town, disappear."

Hearing this man speak about procrastination made everyone give his idea some thought. Thinking something is one thing, saying something is everything. Your words are not only important for your success, but matter more when you are on the road toward success. Just saying "I will" or "I can" makes those dark days, no longer blue.

Your words can also remove barriers too, where locked doors seem impossible to open. So, don't keep asking yourself, why is your life in a holding pattern. Start moving debris out of your vocabulary and just start speaking what you expect to happen and believe it.

When you read the newspaper, or listen to the radio or watch television, you'll notice that there are so many people making their mark in life, right? How is this possible? Do you feel like you are still in a stupor waiting for something amazing to happen to you? Don't you feel like you, too, could be an ice breaker, an inventor or public speaker helping others live better lives?

Examine your latest motto spoken into or over your life lately. Have you shouted openly to the universe, as you take your walk in the park, or along the lake shore, or in the meadows what you expect from yourself, or are you still waiting on someone else to open a pathway in order to make your dreams come into fruition?

If this is you, stop waiting, just say to yourself, I can, I will, and I am. Speak life into your circumstance, situation and into your heart. Wake up! Step on your defeat and beg to differ. Start saying what you will do and not what you are going to do and yes, you will do it. Let's review your last pity party for a moment...who was there? Only you.

When was the last time you just spoke joy, success, peace, happiness over your life? When was the last time you decreed what you will have, what you will do, what will be your next step, or what you are anticipating to abound great in your life?

When you choose to finally speak positivity into your life, remember the past is just that. It's time for new goals, with a new outlook on life. Have you given yourself a time slot, or schedule to reach your new goals? What do you see happening in your life, say in the next year, next month or next week? Do you have any idea what it is you truly want for yourself, your family or humanity? Have you proclaimed your next step?

If you have a vague view of what your next step is going to be, it's time to make some small and maybe, big changes for the new you. Change the dynamics of the future you. Change your conversation with others and mainly within your inner man. Let's get started, right now.

Proclaim It, By Saying It

Just saying one simple word about any subject, releases not only possibility where impossibility once dominated, it also releases endorphins in the brain; stimulating a place where inhibitors of doubt, fear, and hopelessness serve as road blocks.

Just saying empowering words of elevation, inspiration, and encouragement over your dreams, your aspirations are powerful keys to opening new pathways. Don't let your mind lead you to say, "I can't do this," or "I don't think that is possible," or "nothing ever happens great in my life." Leave those unproductive words outside of your thinking patterns and your vocabulary starting RIGHT NOW.

PRACTICE MAKES BETTER

Today you are starting to proclaim new possibilities, remembering the words of Christ who never faded in His purpose or plan for humanity. *"He giveth power to the faint; and to them that have no might He increaseth strength"* (Isaiah 40:29).

When you speak about your greatest fears, your heart slows down, your palms become sweaty, and most of all you become solemn. Weak words weaken your flow leading you to become pitifully discouraged instead of determined or inspired. I always say, never cook after having an intense disagreement with someone, nothing good can come from your heart, because you are frustrated, perplexed and truly not inspired.

You have an innate ability to change the trajectory of

your life, by proclaiming such phrases like "I deserve the best life has to offer," or "*I can do all things through Christ Jesus who strengthens me,*"... *or* "I am a winner," or "I will not be defeated" changes the dynamics of the universe in your favor.

Speaking encouraging words over your life is like taking a cold shower after walking in scorching hot sun for hours. You become renewed, rejuvenated, ready to get going again. By proclaiming what it is you will do in your life, into your life, is like using a new set of keys to opening new doors of opportunities to overtake you. When opportunities begin to come your way, it feels like God sent a bone your way, finally.

Why? Your words carry strong swords with each letter, comment, and idea that enters your mindset, especially when each one comes out of your own mouth. That is why proclaiming your next move, your next step is not only important for your outlook, its critical.

Productivity

WHEN LIFE APPEARS TO BE GETTING THE BEST OF YOU, falling into a slump or becoming depressed is not unusual. Taking one step forward toward getting on your feet, is harder than it seems. It is in these instances you would be less productive than usual. Don't you think if you had spoken of happier times or situations the outcome would be different? The Bible reminds humanity of how powerful, yet detrimental words can be, once they are spoken.

"But now ye also put off all these; anger, wrath, malice, blasphemy, filthy communication out of your mouth" (Colossians 3:8).

No matter what circumstances, thoughts, or ideas that may roam through your head, rather good or indifferent; the result comes into effect once certain words are spoken into the atmosphere. Words are powerful tools when spoken, over, and over again.

The Bible speaks vividly about the power of the tongue. *"Death and life are in the power of the tongue: and they that love it shall eat the fruit thereof"* (Proverbs 18:21).

As written in one of the four gospels, Matthew speaks vividly about your ability to change your destiny through spoken words. *"But those things which proceed; out of the mouth come forth from the heart; and they defile the man"* (Matthew 15:18).

Know earnestly how powerful your own words can be. Your words can make you not only a better player at the table of life, but also, a happier more productive person.

When you speak life into your vocabulary, your words can aide you toward stepping outside of the mundane, into a much more centered life. Why not live a life overflowing in an abundance of love, harmony and productivity?   A life totally expressing happiness and peace to others, where ever you step your feet. When people are in your mist, they begin to feel that you are exhilarated, having renewed joy gleaming from the top of your head to the soles of your feet.

BUILD NEW COURAGE

SPEAKING A BETTER LIFE INTO EXISTENCE, TAKES COURAGE.
Do you have the courage to speak life into the atmosphere daily? You are probably asking yourself, "how does speaking certain words, or phrases have anything to do with courage?" Well, not everyone can speak positive words, daily.

Despite how much drama, discontent, unexpected circumstances or undelightful occurrences that may come about, you can be confident, when you look at the positive instead of the negative. Speaking positive words over all negative forces in your mist, is like cool rain falling on your back on a hot summer day.

It's refreshing, uplifting. Just saying such powerful phrases like "yes I will" or "yes I can" empowers you. The universe seems to smile back at you. What ideas that once appeared out of reach, soon becomes an astounding possibility. You are now feeling enlightened, more confident about life and your journey.

Stand on God's promises. Know He will give you just what you speak into the universe. If you, are bold in your convictions, He will be BOLD in you, too. Courage is standing up for yourself against all that comes before you, that is unlike HIM. For God is all goodness, all greatness, all that is right and brilliantly abundant.

He promised to never leave you nor forsake you. For all things unjust, ill-will, imperfect, stagnant and dark are under His feet. You can stand on those things too, when you exclaim with your mouth, "I am" and "I can" and "I will."

Once you start operating your daily affairs from a place of courage, you will instantly feel empowered more and more. You'll see optimism leading your actions, and your every step. Why? Your own words can give you a new confidence to move with great power and might. Confidence, like courage, can break those chains of despair and defeat that have been beating you down. Your words of confidence can give you a new courage to overcome stagnation and procrastination too.

Your new attitude, your new-found vocabulary can get you geared up to walk bountifully with an optimistic outlook. You will no longer be upset at setbacks or defeats, but, looking forward to ridding all negativity from your path because of what you've just proclaimed – You'll have victory over all your affairs and encounters.

Like King David said in the 23rd Psalm, *"The Lord*

is my shepherd, I shall not want." He proclaimed his destiny, to the Lord.

Your mindset is not easily changed, nor interchanged by mere words. You are human, not a computer. So, you must practice your approach to everyday conversations with confidence. Start examining how you answer average questions. Thinking twice before you speak matters. Think before you make even the smallest of decisions, will help in how you view your destiny.

Over time, your empowering thoughts will become regimented. Those old habits, old ways of thinking negatively, will become minimal, day by day. Your new spoken words are slowly changing, and so are you. Soon, the way you think about small things will diminish, your mind will lead you to thinking on bigger and better life choices.

Try this, the next time you are in a conversation which seems to be swimming toward negativity. Speak life into the conversation. Take the high road, by just saying something as simple as "oh well" or "things will get better" or "expect the best" and see if you don't feel great.

Essentially, because you are no longer letting your mind agree with the negative, your new-found courage gave you a confident answer to everything, spoken, rather you agreed with the conversation or not. You took control of the conversation through exercising a positive perspective on whatever has been said. Your words turned the table around for your good.

After changing the way you speak about your life and your journey, everything becomes enlightened. You are more optimistic, despite circumstances. Now you know that no matter how unfavorable the road ahead appears to be, you can see victory ahead. Why, because your words are igniting new life into all your dreams, hopes and aspirations. Remember you want to always gravitate toward that gigantic positive force of having just what you proclaim, that gallantly moves constantly in the atmosphere. Grab it, it's yours.

Expectation and Faith, Walk Together

EXERCISE YOUR FAITH IN GOD BY EXPECTING GREAT CHANGE for your good. Be bold in your expectations, knowing you can do spectacular work, better than the next person. Speaking bold words of expectation when life seems to chase you down or try to pull you down at the least little thing, can change everything. Choosing to speak up with boldness, with anticipation is a move of faith. Refusing to be backed into a corner, where there seems as if there is no way out is an act that faith.

Use your instinctive abilities to survive as if your life depends on it. By just saying to yourself, in front of a mirror early in the morning, "I will succeed, I cannot fail, I will get this done and that done," moves mountains. Speak out of the innate faith God gave man in the beginning of life. Like when you were a toddler crawling on the floor with baby knees, you knew you could one day stand up, and walk like the big adults walking around you. Soon that first step happened, and you walked.

Expectation has no limits, except the one's you allow to interrupt your plans or dreams. Faith is a perfect tool to use to get you to that place where expectations become a reality. Faith is a thought process fed by your deepest desires, your hopes, your dreams. *"But without faith, it is impossible to please Him..."* (Hebrews 11:6).

When you expect something great to happen in life, you know without a shadow of doubt, it will. That is faith on steroids, but, faith is trusting God despite the odds working against you. Expectation and faith are cousins, holding hands to jump over hurdles that seem too dangerous to cross alone.

When faith and expectation team up, nothing can block the outcome. Operating your mindset with faith and expectation will turn your new-found vocabulary into a giant doorway of possibilities. To that place where anything is possible, simply anything. Speak life into your plans. Know that your faith will carry you and God will do the rest. Faith activates your God given talents, expectation will be there cheering you on.

Expectation says to your sub-conscious, you can rule the world. Remember expectation is a powerful mindset. If you can not see it, if you do not expect it, nor trust yourself to attain it, you will not. Your words, your thoughts and your ideas, hang out together. Make sure you use each one in a positive wonderful way, then watch God meet you there.

God told Moses to lead the slaves out of Egypt. He told God he just minds the sheep, but to God he was a leader. God expected him to do it and told him to do it and well, the rest is history.

Most parents tell their young, they can be anything they set their mind too. Those words are ever so true. When you put something so important on your mind, you usually get it done right? So what is stopping you from walking in devout expectation, knowing you can do anything no matter how impossible it appears to everyone else.

When you lay your head down to rest each night, your plans for the next day are already wondering around in your head. You might have a job interview, a big proposal you are going to present, you might have a big presentation at school, or a medical examination you are anxious about, either way you have expectation to get to tomorrow.

You are already preparing yourself for what awaits you. Expectation is the key to your next day going well, or fantastic. You can "will" your outcome in your mind. Expecting all things to work out as you plan, is a perfect example of expectation.

Patience Through God

Knowing your words are working overtime for your greater good, speak each one with a patient heart. Having patient and peaceful confidence, goes a long way. Remembering you are expecting the best life has to offer, so time is on your side. It is by knowing the best things in life are on your tongue and at your fingertips. Remember its like gulping down a cool refreshment on a sizzling hot summer day. Although, know that all timing is in God's hands. Know that His promises are true. You may speak it, but God brings it too pass. So, by you simply waiting on God, with true patience is a must.

God's will for your life, always comes first. His mighty hand will give you divine instructions on what to do next. It is when you rely on His word, the impossible becomes possible. However, if you do not speak life over your journey, how can a renewed life exist in your affairs or in you? For God gives you what you say, when you get out of His way to bring your deepest desires to surface. *"Be patient and stand firm..."* (James 5:8, NIV).

Waiting on God is sometimes a tedious task for some, and for others, it's an excellent way to get closer to Him, to the light that only illuminates from those who walk closer to the light.

When walking close to the light of life, there are countless benefits, like a renewed mind, a more peaceful demeanor, a joyful continence, a more patient mindset. These qualities are gifts from God. Why? You decided to rely on God's hand because you need His direction to accomplish those wonderful aspirations you have held close to your heart. It wasn't possible until you chose to walk by faith, walk with expectation and just speak life to all your hopes, dreams, even ideas.

"Be like those who through faith and patience will receive what God has promised" (Hebrews 6:12, NCV).

Acting out of patience, knowing your new-found words of inspiration are guiding you toward a more productive and empowered life never fails. Knowing that what you proclaim day in and day out is not only powerful, it is also life changing in more ways than one.

Each tiny moment you apply encouraging words over all that concerns you, transforms your life more and more. Your new vocabulary brings about a new attitude, a new way of thinking about everything and everyone. Your new mindset clears away old cob webs of laziness, procrastination, fear, depression and most of all, doubt.

Leaving solemn thoughts at the gate, works. Never allow impulsive ideas to surface nor sidetrack your expectations. Keep anticipating what you believe to be yours by claiming it daily. Walking by faith is key, toward pleasing God.

You are your greatest advocate. Keep caring for your tomorrows by embracing your plans with great honor, faith and assurance. Remember just speaking it, just shouting it, means decree and declare that thing in which you are believing God to bless you with.

Have faith in not only in your plans, but also in almighty God that is within you. For God knows what life has in store for all creation. You know what your heart thirst for, like no other human on this great earth, but He knows your heart's desire, too. Trust Him to deliver.

"Delight yourself in the Lord, and He will give you the desires of your heart desires" (Psalm 37:4, NKJV).

Be an inspiration not only to yourself, but to those around you. Let others see your dreams coming true, as you walk inspired, with a boldness that exudes a contagious confidence.

When you walk with an overly confident demeanor, whatever you speak over your life, over your dreams and mostly to your inner thoughts...nothing can stop you, nothing.

Speak life over all things, old and new. Do not allow lack of self-esteem, lack of confidence or lack of assurance nail its dart in your daily plans. Stay upbeat, confident, saying bold statements of assurance no matter how uncertain situations or circumstances may seem or appear.

Always take the high road. Leave negative words and torn emotions from entering your mind and conversation. Spend your time wisely, surrounding yourself with people, who too, are confident, assertive, always walking in assurance.

Speaking Empowering Words, Moves Mountains

JUST SPEAKING IT IS MORE THAN AN EXERCISE TO ATTAIN a better life, its a daily effort that only you have control over. Your words are important. When others listen to you, they reflect on who you are in this world. If you use weak, insignificant words in your conversation, that is a profound reflection of you, internally. So why sell yourself short?

You are significant. You have the authority to make or break your next move by exercising a more empowering vocabulary in your profession, your relationships and yes, in your private thoughts. Why not make a change for a better life, a more positive life, by changing the phrases you speak each day.

Listed are words and phrases, which speak life despite circumstances:

I will

I can

I know

I expect

I am

I believe

I will not fail

Failure is not an option

The best is on its way

Things are looking up

It's my time

It's my turn

Today is mine for the asking....

Everything is looking up....

My better days are on the way...

Nothing is going to stop me now....

Every knock is a new door opening before me...

I know my God always has my back...

I can do all things through God who strengthens me...

I'll be promoted, next...

My plans are in motion...

Every one of my goals will succeed...

I'm on my way to higher places...

Using confident words as declarations, instead of negative statements can surely change your life's course. Remember when using empowering phrases, having an assertive conversation, like using upbeat words in your sentences to others you meet on your life journey will be a prime game changer despite the odds.

No matter how late in life, the process of changing how you look at yourself or how you speak about yourself, begins, it really doesn't matter. The main objective in your life is to just speak those deepest desires into reality today because only you can "just speak it" only you!

About the Author

Journalist, Ingrid E. Bridges, for over two decades, is known in Chicago circles as a profound writer with hundreds of powerfully moving articles in the Chicago Defender Newspaper, Chicago Sun-Times, N'Digo Mega paper and Ink Pages.

As one of Chicago's award-winning prized writers and orators of spiritual and interfaith issues. She's featured in numerous books and publications including "Who's Who of Chicago" as a legendary writer and "Spirit-Filled Journey" daily devotional.

Currently, she's co-producer, writer and host of the "According To Ingrid" talk show on CAN–TV, cable network, where Bridges expounds about spirituality on a global scale. The show's topics include everything from "The Mayan Calendar Prophecies of 2012" to "Worldwide Takeover of Islam" to "The War between Religion & Politics." Over a million viewers across Chicago land tune into her show since 2010.

Bridges knack for writing began as a curious youngster wanting to appease her peers in high school as the only Black to serve on student council. It worked, due to her savvy choice of animated skits and plots in her prose. She began writing poetry at the age of 12, but professionally her works started to flourish when the religion section of the Chicago Defender Newspaper was a simple one-page listing.

However, after Bridges took the reins as an editor/writer, the daily newspaper's religion listing became a booming, six-page animated spirit-filled section depicting the rich culture of African American religion and worldwide spirituality. She interviewed movie stars, mainstream, and worldwide religious leaders and wrote hard news and the Life Times section, giving her a chance to explore the sciences, news and personal profiles of everyday people.

When the late Cardinal Joseph Bernadine of the Chicago Catholic Archdiocese, took ill, the news department at the Chicago Defender didn't cover it, but Bridges did. Her professional works include one-on-one interviews with such greats as Tiger Woods, Bruce Willis, Dalai Lama, Ambassador Andrew Young, Oprah Winfrey, Mayo Angelo, Bishop T.D. Jakes, Stedman Graham, Bernie Mac, Minister Louis Farrakhan, Cardinal Francis George, Father Michael Pfleger, and hundreds of others in politics, law, and the arts. She holds over 50 awards and citations for her works as a Journalist.

Bridges expertise in ecumenical and interfaith matters, became a household name in religious and political circles, allowing her to serve in a much big arena politics. She served as the liaison to Chicago's Mayor, Richard M. Daley for 16 years, where she worked in the Mayor's Office as a Special Aid to the Faith & African American Community. Working in numerous capacities, mainly in social, civic and ecumenical circles with senators, congressmen, and (then) with Senator, Barack Obama. Officially speaking on behalf of the Mayor before leaders of the interfaith community–African American, Jewish, Buddhist, and Muslim–to build capacity, and enhance relationships within the entire ecumenical community. Bridges was designated to create and write the first "Youth Resource Guide" ever published by the City of Chicago.

Currently, her mission to create, inform and entertain the masses continues in a sea of diverse books known to inspire and uplift those who read her prose. She is also working on completing "Church Lady" about her journey as a reporter in Chicago's huge religious community.

Among her latest literary works is a book entitled, "Just Speak It" (God is listening) depicts what happens when a person chooses to change their course in life toward empowerment and renewed self-esteem. A quick read.

About the Publisher

Let us bring your story to life! With Life to Legacy, we offer the following publishing services: manuscript development, editing, transcription services, ghostwriting, cover design, copyright services, ISBN assignment, worldwide distribution, and eBook production and distribution.

Throughout the entire production process, you maintain control over your project. We also specialize in family history books, so you can leave a written legacy for your children, grandchildren, and others. You put your story in our hands, and we'll bring it to literary life! We have several publishing packages to meet all your publishing needs.

Call us at: 877-267-7477, or you can also send e-mail to: Life2Legacybooks@att.net. Please visit our Web site:

www.Life2Legacy.com